HOW TO RETIRE

THE WORKING PERSON'S GUIDE TO A GOOD RETIREMENT
HOW THE WORKING CLASS RETIRES

MONTY BONDS
J. BONDS

NEWMAN SPRINGS PUBLISHING
320 Broad Street
Red Bank, NJ 07701

First originally published by Newman Springs Publishing 2024

ISBN 979-8-89061-856-6 (Paperback)
ISBN 979-8-89061-857-3 (Digital)

Printed in the United States of America

INTRODUCTION

There are lots of books and writings out there for you to study. My goal with this book is to break down some of the basic, simple things that are practical and easy to understand. Also, by reading this book, it's my hope that it will refresh your mind and get you to refocus on those things that you can do.

I am neither a genius nor an expert at finances. I am not a financial planner or advisor, or any expert on money, wealth, and finances. What I do know is that over the years, I've learned many things. I started late. You've heard the old saying, when you're young, you just don't know what all you don't know. That is so true. And when I was young and just starting out as a worker, I wasted a lot of money and good advice that I received from those who were wiser than me. But that was also when I thought I knew everything. Boy, was I wrong.

So do get professional advice from someone you feel you can trust. If you don't mind paying a few dollars up front, then I would suggest you see a fee-only-type financial advisor. They have no incentive to try to talk you into buying products you may not need. A lot of other financial advisors will try to talk you into buying products, mostly because they make a commission from them.

What you read and learn is not worth a red cent to you if you don't apply it. So everything in this book is based on life's experiences. Things that I've gone through, seen, and learned from family and friends and the experiences they've gone through over the years.

So whether or not you take anything away from this book, or any other things you study, is entirely up to you. But always remember, no one, I mean no one, has the potential to look after you like you do.

So read, enjoy, and move yourself forward.

Thank you.

Notes

CHAPTER 1

The million-dollar question: Can an average working person still retire comfortably? The short answer is yes. Yes, you can retire, and retire comfortably if you really want to. But the most truthful answer is that most people probably won't make much effort to accumulate much in the way of money to have a comfortable, worry-free retirement. Most will continue to do the same things, living the same lifestyle, making the same day-to-day bad decisions they have been making. Guess what, nothing will change for them. Are you in this group?

Most of you will continue to work hard, continue to just barely get by. You're just working week by week. Each pay period, you are waiting on your next paycheck. You are hoping that you will have enough money to make it till your next paycheck comes in. Don't let your retirement end up this same way. You don't have to unless you choose to.

If you are one of those thinking, "Maybe one day, I'll win the lottery," then we will have enough money to live comfortably and even have that retirement we've always dreamed of. Well, if you are one of those that believe that, then welcome to the stupid club.

There truly is not some magic or easy button that automatically gives you your comfortable retirement. If you are working for someone, then hopefully they are withholding and paying in your social security taxes. This will give you some income in your later years, if the government can continue to fund the program. But most of the time, this doesn't give you enough monthly income to enjoy much of an active retirement lifestyle. But we will discuss this later.

The percentage of people in this world that actually accumulate much wealth and don't have to put much effort into it is a very small number of people. Because there's something about earning what you have that seems to make you not waste it, makes you cherish it, but it also makes you respect yourself better. I didn't want to be one of those wasting my time and talents, hoping someone would provide for me. I wanted to be assured that my family and I would have enough to survive on.

So are you going to be one of those that are dumb enough to just sit around and hope that a large sum of money just drops from the sky and forever changes your life, or are you going to make the decision today? Tell yourself that you are going to put the effort into taking charge of your life today.

To get ahead in this world, most of the effort is not only putting in more hard work or longer hours, but just as important, it's the effort you put into it with your heart and your head. If you're not going to at least make a solid decision today, and really mean it, to put your life on the path to a better tomorrow, then you might as well forget all about it. Without this commitment from you, you won't have much of a chance of reaching your potential. So if you want to continue to belong to the stupid club, then just keep on doing what most people are already doing, which is just averagely getting by.

This world is full of dumb, lazy people—yes, lazy. That is a weakness in character that has been taught and handed down, sometimes from generation to generation. This weakness has been accepted as normal by a growing number of people. Some lazy people just want someone else to do all the hard work and give them some of their hard-earned money because they are just too lazy to put much effort into making it themselves. And if you are one of these lazy people, then odds are you will not be successful in anything you do, and you shouldn't be. Some unmotivated people are not content to live as they are, unless someone gives them something to make their lazy precious lives better, and that is not okay. Why is it fair to those that work hard to provide and make this world a better place, to have to give a portion of their hard-earned money to someone that is just lazy and unmotivated?

Rewards should be for those that try to make their lives and the lives of others better.

So right now, make that decision. Decide, "Am I too lazy to make the effort and use my resources and talents to better myself? Am I too dumb to see that I need to make this effort on my own, and not just sit around hoping that a big bag of money will somehow drop out of the sky into my lap and all my money worries will miraculously be solved?"

Notes

Now, let's start by being clear about one thing. Success is truly measured in several ways. My idea of having a successful life is belonging to and being a part of a happy family. Building and being part of a good family does also take lots of effort and hard work. But it is well worth it in the long run.

Some measure wealth in feeling good about themselves and how they handle themselves, and no doubt this is also a great wealth to have. You need to have confidence in yourself. You will never ever know everything. You will never make every decision 100 percent correctly. But you can feel good about the effort you are making. Standing still and letting everyone else go on by isn't a good life's strategy. If you are making the effort. Are you?

Some measure their wealth by the job or career they are working toward. A great job or career is something to be proud of if you really enjoy what you do. But also, your career should be helping you to reach your retirement goals. You can make lots of money and not do the right thing with it, but you will not reach your full potential. Then you just created and become part of a lost opportunity.

But for the purpose of this book, we will focus on the money side of wealth. Which, in my opinion, is the least valuable of all the things that seem to make us feel wealthy. In particular, we will focus on the minor steps and commitment you need to take to have a comfortable retirement for you and your family. So if you belong to the millions and millions of working-class people that help keep this world's economy going, then it's you that we're having this discussion with. Always know that it takes all of us, in all classes of workers and people, to keep this world's economy going. But without a doubt, it is you, the working men and women of this world, that keep the stores and businesses going. Without us, the working class, the economy would fail.

So read and enjoy my straightforward way of discussing this with you. But most of all, start, start today. Don't do like a lot of others will do and a lot of others have already done. And I'm sure you've heard this many a time, procrastination is one of the biggest mistakes when it comes to planning for retirement. Don't let yourself wake up one morning and realize it's too late to do much with your retirement. Then you have to change strategies and play catchup fast. You are better than that. You can do this. It starts with a decision you make to yourself. Make that decision, make it right now.

So if you're still reading this book, then that probably means you don't want to be one of those that are dumb and lazy, and you want more out of this life. Remember, retirement planning is not just about learning to budget. Even though budgeting is an important part of daily living. It's just a fact: those that live by and maintain a budget most of the time end up doing better off financially in the long run.

There's something that I heard someone say that I will always remember. I heard this after I had gone through a portion of my life making those unwise decisions. That's when I thought I knew everything, but in reality, I didn't have enough common sense or vision to make those solid decisions that I should have. And I'm still dumb and trying to grow in knowledge and common sense every day. These words of wisdom I heard and realized that they just may be true, so I took them to heart. These words of wisdom are something I'm sure you've heard countless times. If you want to improve yourself, then start improving your mind and your heart. Then only—and I mean *only*—listen to and watch positive things that push you to constantly think, plan, and develop your mind to a better place. Your mind and body are only what you feed into them. Invest in them, just as you would invest in anything you felt was important to you.

Invest not only your time but also your willingness and your eagerness to learn and develop yourself.

The same with your heart, only associate or hang around those that have a good heart, those that help you be wiser, more forgiving, kinder when it is needed, but firm when someone or something is trying to steer you in a direction that is not good for you. Without a good and wise heart and a good sense of life's direction, it's hard to keep straight on what's really right and wrong. In today's times, it's very easy to get influenced by others into going in the wrong direction. You be the one that's in charge of you.

Read—read things that will improve not only your knowledge of the things you are involved in but also let you feel more comfortable with the direction you are taking in your life. Remember every decision you make or don't make can be critical. Again, always remember your mind and heart are made up of what you put in it. These are all things that only you can do. If you have the true desire to improve yourself, then you can and should. But if you aren't willing to make the effort, then not much else can be said.

I started reading and listening to motivational and financial items and without a doubt, over time it has completely changed my life, especially the motivational items. The positive outlook on things became the one thing I could always count on. It not only changed the way I thought about things, but it also changed the decisions I was making. It made me feel more confident about the direction I was going in.

Notes

CHAPTER 3

Alright, so now you've made that decision to start your life on a different course. What do I do next? Well, let's start by answering a basic question. How much will you actually need in retirement? There are lots of people trying to give you advice on this. But beware of those giving advice who are not retired yet themselves. I'm one of those who believe that if you haven't been there, then you don't really know what it's like. They just give advice based off of things they have read or have been told and taught.

Lots of financial people will tell you that you will only need about 75 percent of your working income during your retirement years. That may be so if you're willing to scale back your lifestyle after you retire. But in reality, most people don't really want to do this unless they have to. Are you wanting to reduce your lifestyle when you retire?

Some will say that there will be expenses while you are working that you won't have in retirement.

That is partially true. But on the other hand, there will probably be other expenses that you will have in retirement that you did not have while you were working.

The laws of nature say, because you are aging, that you will have more medical and medicine expenses as you age. You may even find that you will end up hiring a few more things done around your home and vehicle as you age, than you did when you were younger. You may even want to travel more, spend time and money on kids and grandkids. Everyone's health will be different in their later years, everyone's hobbies and lifestyles will be different. Even you yourself don't really know for sure what your situation will be.

Inflation will definitely affect you over time. Social Security COLA adjustments (cost of living adjustments) on your social security are always a year late. This is the raise everyone on Social Security receives every year. These COLA adjustments or raises are generally not enough to cover the actual cost of inflation for seniors.

Taxes will have a very negative impact on your retirement and lifestyle. Study them, get to know as much as possible about them. Run calculations, do the math, see how much extra you will need to save or have for your retirement to pay your taxes. You will need to minimize the negative and possibly devastating impact of taxes and inflation.

The government is not your friend in retirement. And because governments in general are large, ever-growing, money-craving monsters, they will continue to drain from you as much of your hard-earned money as they think you'll give up. So become tax smart, plan for it, save for it. Don't do like most people and wait till you start retirement, and get shocked at how much your retirement savings gets reduced, potentially even your social security check.

Things to really think about hard before doing them. Reverse mortgages, in my opinion, are not a good financial move, unless you are truly in need of money with no other way. Only consider something like this once you have talked to a financial advisor. Make sure these financial advisors don't sell these products themselves. Use someone completely independent to advise you.

Annuities, right now annuities are the talk of the town. Again in my opinion, from a financial standpoint, they are not a wise investment. There are lots of people trying to talk everyone into buying these annuities. But most of those trying to talk you into buying an annuity stand to make money themselves from you on commissions from these products. Only consider something like this if it gives you an easy, comfortable feeling knowing that your money or a portion of it is not dependent on the stock markets, etc. Know that the institutions that are issuing you these annuities usually have very high fees. Also, there are usually limitations on you being able to pass some of these annuities onto your heirs. Again, talk to an independent financial agent that doesn't sell or get a commission from these products and verify they agree that this is the right product for you to buy into.

I don't know of anyone that has already retired that believes they saved too much or have too much money in their retirement accounts, nobody.

Start by doing the little things. If you work for someone else, that's fine, most of us do. There will always be millions and millions of people that don't want the pressures of working for themselves, or the extra amount of hard work and long hours it takes to work in your own business. Even if you're thinking about working in your own business, don't think about it long if you're not ready to work a lot harder, put in a lot more hours than you would if you were typically working for someone else. Very few small businesses will be successful unless you are willing to put in the extra hours and hard work, and for the long haul. Then it can still be a struggle to make them successful. But if all goes well and you stay steady at it, then you stand a chance to be more financially successful by working in your own business.

Notes

CHAPTER 4

Always remember, you hear a lot of people giving advice to you about making the correct decision on the one or two big decisions that come your way in your lifetime. And those are important. The ones that could potentially change your life for good, but you're just not sure. For instance, taking that new job offer, should I or shouldn't I? Sometimes these decisions are tough to make, but go back to your heart and use your brain. Will this new job help me or hurt me in accomplishing my life's goals? Will I be happy at this new job? There's an old saying, "Don't let a shiny nickel trick you into doing something stupid." Meaning, don't get sucked into a job that looks or sounds good on the surface, but doesn't help you reach your goals, or is something you won't enjoy doing. But if it seems right for you, then do it with confidence, go into whatever you've chosen with everything you have, no fear, no regrets, just wide open and expecting great things.

But as important as those big decisions are, I truly believe more importantly, it's the small day-to-day decisions that will define your direction and success. Don't make small daily idiotic decisions that are not financially or morally sound. Don't blow good money on junk and trash items that you don't truly need. Don't charge on any credit cards that you can't or don't pay off every month before interest is charged. Like most wise financial people will say, you just can't get ahead when your finances are having to overcome those high interest rates. Just don't do it. If you're not disciplined enough to pay them off in full each month, then you're better off not using them. Don't put yourself in a situation where you are tempted or find it convenient to charge to a credit card.

Moving on, don't overspend on expensive vehicles, eating out at fancy restaurants, or anything that puts you in a financial strain. You don't have to never have any enjoyment in life, just use good common sense in your judgment. Making the right decisions and doing the right thing with the money you have at the earliest possible time in your life makes all the difference, and what a difference, it will make in your retirement.

Never ever listen to or follow what you know may be bad advice. I once heard a financial guy who was working at one of the large banks give a talk to a small group of people. He told them that there was no need to ever contribute more than 10 percent to their retirement plans. That was stupid advice, but he was still pretty naive and hopefully his brain started working before he gave out too much more advice. It is very unlikely you will ever save too much for retirement.

Always keep good food and shelter for you and your family. Just be truly smart about your spending and savings. This is something you will definitely look back on when you retire and thank your younger self for having the discipline and the willpower to begin planning for your retirement when you did.

You, yourself, work and contribute to this world. Be a positive influence and example to others. Help make this a better place for the next generation and teach this next generation to also teach and be a positive example and influence to the generation after them.

But let's say, for instance, you are more comfortable working for someone else. What can I do to get ahead and have a better retirement?

So take these few words of wisdom and use them. Start today. But if you want to be foolish and live like those that are living like crazy idiots, then just go ahead, keep doing it. There's always room for those that don't want a better life in this society. But if you're thinking you don't have to make any effort and that society or the governments will eventually take care of you, then you just may be lazy and a blooming idiot. Because for any government to take care of the few that truly need it, then it takes a lot of daily workers contributing their taxes to those funds to support those few that are truly in need of the help.

But to be perfectly clear, there are those in this society that do truly need and deserve extra help from either their families or their governments. Those that truly deserve to be helped should receive those benefits provided by their governments by and through the people that support their governments through their taxes. But if over time fewer and fewer workers are working and contributing their taxes, whether it's because of an aging population dropping out of the workforce or just too many people trying to get onto the system and get as much free stuff as they can, then over time there will not be any or enough funds to support not only those that are truly in need, nor will the governments be able to provide for those that are lazy and just want their governments and the taxpayers to also provide for all their needs and wants. So don't be lazy, don't be a thief and take those benefits if you can physically or mentally work to provide for yourself. If you don't make an effort to provide for yourself, then you are stealing benefits and funds from those in need and those that are working hard to support those funds and programs by contributing into the system.

So what do I need to do to get started? Now if you're working for someone else, that's great. Start today, become the very best and the most valuable employee at your workplace. This will not only help you keep your job during tough times but will also help you during times of layoffs. You will also be more apt to get promotions and pay raises. This does not usually mean a lot more physical work, but mostly a change in attitude. Become smart enough to know what your employer needs of you and provide and excel in it. Outperform everyone else. Don't ever try to make someone else look or perform their duties badly, not ever. This would defeat your purpose and eventually it could come back against you. Be humble and courteous at all times.

I once heard an employer tell one of their employees that they had improved so much that they had become one of their best employees. And because of your efforts, it has definitely made all of the other employees even better, just from the example that you have set for everyone. That's the kind of employee you want to become. Do you think this person was ever laid off or passed up for promotion? No.

Notes

CHAPTER 5

Okay, next, whether or not you think you can, you can. Contribute to your employer's 401(k) or similar plan if they have one. Remember the old wise saying, always pay yourself first. Contribute as much as you can. Your lifestyle will adjust and probably won't change one bit. Then about every six months or so, if your plan allows, bump your contribution percentage up at least 1 percent. Keep doing this until you eventually max out your contributions allowed by federal law every year. Don't stop or pause your contributions because you think you need the money to buy a new car or take the family on a big expensive vacation. Find another way to fund your purchases. Again, always pay yourself first and never stop. You can be smart enough to fund your purchases without damaging your future retirement money, or you will decide to postpone those purchases until you can afford them. Always remember and learn, it's not just only the amount of money you save every year, it's also that com-pounding effect and growth that happens every year over time that makes your money grow. A very famous person once said that compounding inter-est was the greatest invention ever thought up. Most financial professionals would agree. Do the math; it really does work. But also being in the stock markets or some types of investment accounts have proven over the last century to be the best place to park your money for the long run, if you want your money to grow. Now the markets do go up and down, but over the years, they have proven to grow wealth, and we have no reason to believe it will change, for now anyway. But always either study and learn yourself your investment choices or discuss with someone you trust to advise you and help guide you on what types of investments are right for you. Money in checking and savings accounts just in reality lose money every year due to inflation unless you are drawing an incredible amount of interest. Money held in these types of accounts should only be for daily living, short-term emergency funds, or anything you will be needing to withdraw money from quickly.

Then after you've learned to max out your 401(k) every year, start also and max out a Roth IRA. Do not stop contributing to your 401(k), do both. Do the Roth at a separate institution than your employer's 401(k). Max out your contributions for both of these. Then I know I'm pushing you, and it seems like I'm asking a lot out of you, but if you can spare just a few more dollars on top of these, then contribute to a personal IRA. Again, this will be with another institution outside your employer's 401(k).

Again, if you do all this, your older self will thank your younger self for doing this. Don't worry about saving too much, you won't. The average person in retirement does not feel very comfortable with the amount of money they have. Most wish they had done better with their retirement saving. You want to feel relaxed and comfortable when you do retire. So by doing these things early enough, you can be better off than the average person entering into retirement.

If you don't have access to a 401(k), then go straight into a Roth. Max it out as early in the year as you can. If you have a working spouse, then have them max theirs out as early in the year as possible also. Then also start contributing to a personal IRA. Place as much money in this every year as possible. Check with a financial advisor on how much you can contribute to these types of accounts each year. I can't overstate how important it is for you to max out these accounts as early as you legally can each and every year. And start early if at all possible.

Learn and study about the negative effects of taxes in retirement. They will have a negative impact on you and your money in retirement and can affect your lifestyle. Most employer-sponsored 401(k) plans are not taxed before you contribute into your 401(k). Meaning, you will pay taxes on this money as you draw it out during your retirement. But you have been allowed to use the money that would have normally gone to taxes, to be placed in your 401(k) and grow, either in stocks, bonds, interest-bearing accounts, or whatever investment you have it in. Again, just an interesting sidenote, checking accounts, savings accounts, or CDs are not a good place to park long-term money in. Once you study the small amount of interest you are making in these accounts versus inflation, you will better understand that typically you are steadily losing money each year with these types of accounts. Like most financial advisors will tell you, and I am not one of them, only keep money's that you may need in the short term or emergency money in these types of accounts.

So in most 401(k)s, you won't pay taxes until you start withdrawing, but on most Roths, you pay your taxes before you contribute and therefore, you won't pay any taxes when you do withdraw. Which can be a good thing. This could become very beneficial to you when you start withdrawing money from your retirement accounts after you retire. Just a reminder that if you start withdrawing money from some retirement accounts too early, there could be penalties and taxes for early withdrawals. Federal law says, with a few exceptions, that you can't withdraw from certain types of retirement accounts until you are at least 59 1/2 years old as of this writing. Study and get to know all the plans you're involved with and exactly what the laws allow. Talk to a financial advisor that you trust. And when you do start withdrawing from these types of accounts correctly, it could potentially save you lots of money in taxes. Which means you get to keep more of your savings. This is not just for the wealthy; this is for you, the working person, to take advantage of and use. So use it. We've discussed 401(k) and Roths. Now let's talk IRAs. IRAs are different; they are taxed before you contribute and can also be taxed when withdrawn, and possibly you'll have to pay taxes on the capital gains you make off the money. But all three are well worth it in the long run.

Next, and while you are still working, pay off any and all debt. Try to pay off all debt as early in life as you possibly can. It's tough going into retirement with debt. If it's financially possible, make all large purchases while you are still working, and pay them off with earned working money, not retirement money.

Let's keep going. As early as possible, start thinking about and creating multiple streams of revenue or passive income to tap into after you retire. This will help supplement your Social Security and your savings. Most employers no longer offer a pension plan at your workplace. Therefore, you may be 100 percent dependent on your Social Security and any savings you may have. Who even knows if Social Security will even exist when you retire, and even if it does, the benefits may or may not be reduced. Then your savings and any passive income may make up a greater percentage of your income in retirement. Don't be scared or worried; you can do this. So you can see why it's important to start thinking about and planning for some type of passive or after-retirement income. It could make up a good portion of the money you and your family live off of in retirement. Even a slow start early enough has the potential to grow into enough money to assist you in your retirement years. One of the things that most people in retirement fear is running out of money before they die or not having enough to take care of them in their old age. Even small amounts, like a few hundred dollars a month, can make a huge difference to some in their later years. And if you can duplicate these small amounts of income several times each month, then it can add up to really make a positive difference in your retirement lifestyle. Most people will not put much thought into creating multiple streams of revenue while they are young or still working. And different people have ideas on different types of ways to create these revenue streams. You may feel more comfortable or knowledgeable working on something that is entirely different than that of your coworker or family and friends. That's okay, find and work on what you feel comfortable doing. But keep in mind that even if you say now, "Well, I feel like working till I'm seventy or so," or "I think that I really like what I'm doing, I'll probably just work till I can't work no more," but when you actually get close to retirement age, your health or other circumstances may force you to reconsider retiring earlier than you had previously planned. Most people have a completely different mindset when they get near retirement age than they did years earlier.

I'm just going to list a few of many of the most common things that people do to generate this extra income as of this writing. We'll not go into great detail on these. Let your imagination do that work for you. For the most part, there are no limits and nothing is impossible.

Some take on part-time jobs in retirement. But you can't bank on this being a reality. Who knows if your health or family circumstances will allow you to work during retirement.

You might possibly turn a hobby into a profitable part-time job. Work at your own pace, make a few dollars or make a lot, it would be up to you. Again, your health or family circumstances could affect or limit this.

Some buy property during their working years, hold onto it till just before or during retirement, build up the equity, and then sell and use the extra money to fund their lifestyle. This is usually a good option for those that don't want to do anything hands-on, like rental property. If you purchased land and don't want to sell, then you might have the option to rent the land out to farmers, hunters, etc. Keep in mind you will still be responsible for property taxes and upkeep on the property throughout the years you own it.

Rental property is a very common way to create income and build equity. This is great if you can handle the hard work and sometimes stress of dealing with renters and keeping it rented and maintained. Only do this if you feel comfortable and think you can learn the business and make it profitable. It is a growing industry in our society and is expected to grow over the next several years.

Recheck previous workplaces for old 401(k)s, old pensions, profit sharing, ESOP plans, etc. It's rare, but it has been known for people to go back and find forgotten money. Remember, even small amounts can make a difference.

REITs are another possible option. This allows you to invest and be involved in the housing or building markets without having any hands-on involvement. They are easy to invest in and thanks to legislation, anyone with a few dollars can start investing in them.

Again, as mentioned before, annuities are typically, in my opinion, not a good investment avenue to use. They typically come with very high fees and sometimes have limitations on your ability to pass this money onto your heirs. In my opinion, the main reason I think someone might consider buying an annuity is if they just can't handle the stress of having money in the stock markets or other investments that tend to move up or down. But if you don't mind paying high fees and taking a chance on an insurance company or investment company being solid and financially strong enough to keep paying out all their obligations when you retire and staying financially strong throughout your retirement, then go talk to a financial advisor that does not sell these types of products and get their advice first. Don't go to a financial advisor that sells these products.

Some people are turning to reverse mortgages for extra income in retirement. Again, in my opinion, these are not good investment tools unless you just absolutely don't have another option. Again, talk to a financial expert on this. Don't go to a financial person that sells these types of products either. Like annuities, they have a financial incentive to sell these types of products to you. They make a commission from these, so sure they will tell you that this would be good for you. But again, they come with high fees.

Dividends are another way you hear a lot of noise about when it comes to making extra passive income. But know that it takes money, commitment, and a lot of time to create this into a revenue stream.

As of this writing, there are numerous ways to create extra income or perform work using the internet. Some are legit and many are scams and a waste of your time and money. Beware, a lot of those that advertise these easy ways to make money on the side are trying to get something from you.

There are many other types of things you can do to create revenue in retirement. Use your imagination. But whatever you are thinking about, start early. Don't wait till you're treading water in the middle of the lake before you realize you wish you were closer to the shoreline. Don't make life any harder than it already has to be. Don't live stressed out. And remember the shiny nickel: don't get talked into wasting your good time or money on dumb ideas or gimmicks that are too good to be true. Again, put yourself above things like this. Be solid with your work, your planning, and your ethics. And if you do, then your retirement and your lifestyle will stand a better chance of providing for you and your family. You've got this if you want it.

Notes

Now let me run a crazy scenario by you. Let's say you're young, you're contributing to your 401(k), your Roth, and your IRA. You're also paying off all your debt. You are doing great things, you're headed in the right direction. Let's look at something that may sound crazy, but will potentially give you extra monthly income when you need it in retirement. As an example, think about this. Let's say you're twenty-two years old or whatever age you currently are and you don't have any extra money to invest, because you're investing in all the items mentioned before. Do this, if possible, in January take on a part-time job above and beyond your regular job. Work and save at least $3,000, then quit for the year, if you wish. Invest the $3,000 plus in another IRA. By the time you reach your midsixties, this $3,000 should on average grow to an average of about $50,000. The industry standard for the stock market is that your money approximately doubles about every ten years. Then in retirement, you can start withdrawing about 4–5% on a monthly basis or about $200. By withdrawing approximately 4–5% annually, again the industry standard says your savings money probably will outlast you. Meaning you probably won't run out of money before you die. That doesn't seem like much, but it does help. Now let's continue. You repeat this for the next nine years. Work just enough to make about $3,000 or a little more, invest the money each year. This gives you ten years of extra money to invest and about thirty to thirty-five years plus of investing time. Just imagine ten times plus or minus the $200 each month. This small amount of work while you are young can completely change your lifestyle in retirement. You can quit after ten years or keep on working, it's up to you. I have known people that were determined to improve their financial situation that they continued to work a part-time job year around and throughout their younger years. What a difference it did make in their later years.

Anyways, these are just a few of the most common ways to create extra income. But like most investments, you need to plant these seeds as early as possible. Remember the power of time and growth.

Again, there are numerous ways to create revenue streams. Explore and think about them. Be creative, come up with something you think you can start early and will enjoy. They can really make a difference in your life.

Also, something to take into consideration is the rising cost of things as you get older and actually how much you may need by the time in the future when you do think about retirement. These numbers may have to be adjusted for you to cover the extra cost of inflation by the time you do retire. And always check with a good financial advisor that you trust to verify everything we have discussed.

For your financial sake, don't be foolish, don't put off starting this. Time is worth just as much as money is. I hear people all the time say, "Well, I just can't save much right now. I'm trying to raise a family. I'll start or increase my savings and do better when my kids are out of school, or after my career takes off and I'm making more money." That's foolish, foolish thinking. Even small amounts when you're younger over time makes great strides. It also creates a habit and a pattern that will be much easier for you to follow and maintain.

Even if you are not fortunate enough to have youth and time on your side, start anyway, start now. Everything you do starting today will make a positive impact on you and your family's retirement lifestyle. Not doing anything or postponing things will definitely have a negative impact on your future.

Notes

So let's recap for a minute. Make your decisions now. Don't use credit cards without paying them completely off every month. Become the very best employee at your workplace if you choose to work for someone else. Start to work in your own business, if you think you have the strength and determination to stay with it.

Contribute to your 401(k) or similar plan if your employer offers one. Then, very quickly max out your yearly contributions allowed by federal law. Some people even max out their yearly contributions by around September. This gives them some extra spending money through the holidays without being tempted to use your credit cards. But be sure you restart these contributions at the beginning of each year; don't delay. Contribute and max out your Roth IRAs every year. Be sure to keep your Roth IRAs at another institution separate from your 401(k). Contribute to your individual IRA. There is not as much tax advantage to these as there are with your 401(k) and Roth. But this extra savings will help you out in your retirement.

Some people want to retire a couple of years earlier than average due to declining health or family members' declining health. Maybe even to accomplish some big plan you may have for your retirement years. But they can't because they are scared or afraid they won't have enough money to comfortably retire on. This is very common among those nearing retirement. It's a feeling you want to avoid if at all possible.

But if by some chance you do retire and have accumulated more money than you need, then congratulations. That's very rare, but it's a good feeling. But you do have the opportunity to pass it on to family members. Or you can donate to your favorite charities or causes that you believe in. If planned correctly, no money will go to waste. But believe me, it will definitely take lots more money in retirement than you plan for or think. Things will come up. Unexpected living expenses, unexpected medical that can drain lots of your savings very fast. So don't worry about over-saving; you probably won't.

In closing, this is definitely something you can do for you and your family. Create the freedom you want and deserve. Empower yourself, ensure your retirement is on track. Don't ignore what you've

just read. It all starts with you, your belief in yourself, your dedication to your purpose.

So enjoy life, do good, be kind, be wise, and be
faithful to yourself.

Live well!

Notes

www.ingramcontent.com/pod-product-compliance
Lightning Source LLC
Chambersburg PA
CBHW031003180726
47993CB00018B/1543